I0166506

THE GREAT KIVA

INDIAN MOONLIGHT SONG

THE GREAT KIVA

A POETIC CRITIQUE OF RELIGION

BY PHILLIPS KLOSS

With Etchings By Gene Kloss

THE
SUN
STONE
PRESS

SANTA FE, NEW MEXICO

FIRST EDITION
Copyright © 1980 by Phillips Kloss

All Rights Reserved.
No part of this book may be reproduced in any form
or by any electronic or mechanical means
including information storage and retrieval systems
without permission in writing from the publisher,
except by a reviewer
who may quote brief passages in a review.

Printed in the United States of America

Library of Congress Cataloging in Publication Data

Kloss, Phillips Wray, 1902—
    The great kiva.

    I. Title.
PS3521.L65G7   811'.5'2   79—21344

ISBN 0-913270-82-2 (Hard Cover)
ISBN 0-913270-84-9 (Soft Cover)

Published in 1980 by The Sunstone Press.
Post Office Box 2321 / Santa Fe, New Mexico 87501
United States of America

CONTENTS

THE MECHANISTIC MULTIVERSE

Absorb the night, the night sky, see
Star beyond star beyond infinity
The mechanism of the multiverse reflected in the mechanism of the mind
Like an ant-heap reflecting the star-heap neither cruel nor kind
Microcosm and macrocosm interlinked, intercurled
Except insofar as the miracle of thought,
Seeking a freedom the stars never sought,
Creates its own world.

Structure without stricture, no zodiac strings
Bind the ephemeral flight as of butterfly wings
And when nought that became thought again becomes nought
Absorbed in the night it absorbed standing stoic,
In the night in the dead dynamic stardust caught
Proterozoic.

THE GREAT KIVA

The great kiva at Chetro Ketl in Chaco Canyon, the broken slabstone
walls of the pueblo ruin and massive walls of the sandstone cliff
behind it,
A huge circular pit dug deep in the rocky ground, lined with slab
and block stones, altars of heavier stones set inward, disks for
pillar support set in stone wells,
Excavated by our best archaeologists, left roofless exposed to what-
ever interpretation you wish to impute to it, the mystery of it
haunts you, the primitive feeling of it, meaning of it.
Say it represents the womb of earth, the cave of darkness from which
man emerged into the light, sipapu the outlet, say it contained
the beliefs, the cosmology of a vanished people.
Who were they, where did they come from, why did they leave, where
did they disappear to, Taos, Tsiping, Zuñi, Ácoma, what kind of
god did they worship?
Fragmentary inferences can't be put together like shards of a shat-
tered bowl, but we judge by the beliefs of pueblo peoples today
and we know their religion was benign.
The well-being of the individual, of the tribe, of nature itself was
the purpose of the kiva, invisible spirits, ancestor spirits en-
tered therein to guide and perpetuate.
Compare the cruel gods of Inca, Maya, and Aztec religions to the
friendly spirits of kiva peoples,
Compare the doctrines and dogmas of the Christian churches, the in-
quisitions and persecutions, to the protective superstitions of
kiva peoples,
Compare their self-sufficient way of life to any other, the head men
had to work with the earth like everybody else, plant their own
corn, hunt their own meat, make their own clothes.
Glorification of their culture is fallible, no culture perfect, no
perfection an analogy for imitation.
It is the setting here that grips you, haunts you, inspires you, that
a people chose to settle in such beautiful barrenness and conform
to it so esthetically,
The whole canyon a sipapu for the soul, walk up it to the ponderosa
pines on the continental divide, the circular kiva of the sky above
you, beauty all around you.

EVE OF THE GREEN CORN CEREMONY

DIALECTICAL MATERIALISM

Dialectical spiritualism and dialectical materialism are equivalent
    in compulsion of belief.
Torquemada tortured infidels with iron spikes, iron stretcher chains,
    iron weights.
Lenin chopped off the hands of Russian princesses with hatchets and
    meat cleavers, mowed down dissenters with machine guns.
The sungod Incas controlled every economic phase of human existence,
    enslaved the able-bodied worker to a pre-set job.
Pray a real religion will emancipate the church and state
From cruel convictions.
Morality's the victor, its dialectic stricter.

PREDESTINATION

Perhaps there is a prefixed fate for all the stars
But is it ours?
What satisfaction is there in a virtuous deed
If destiny won't pay the slightest heed?
It doesn't matter anyhow since we
Use words to trap ourselves and words to free.
The earth may wobble off its beaten track,
Elude the signs of the zodiac.
The polar axis may become the equatorial belt,
Heaven change to hell just to feel how it felt.
Plant the corn and hoe the weed,
Determine what we really need.

THE SUNGOD HUITZILOPOCHTLI

The sunpriest stands over the man on the stone
Plunges the knife beneath his breast bone
Rips out his heart and holds it still beating
Up to the sungod for hot-mouthed eating
The bloodthirsty deity Huitzilopochtli.

Drown the young maiden in the deep pool
Religious human sacrifice really isn't cruel
The image of the sun will take her in the water
And perpetuate the people, so give another daughter.
Damned devout delusions deceiving everyone,
There isn't any sungod, the sun is the sun!

SONG OF CREATION

THE REFRIGERATED CORPSE OF LENIN

Did he ever climb a mountain, ever see a gentian, ever listen to a
    birdsong?
Did he ever build a house, ever plough a field, ever do a lick of
    manual work?
His ideology blinded him, deafened him, deadened him, his corpse re-
    frigerated in a glass showcase now.
He wrote a book on Marxism titled *Materialism and Empirio-Criticism*
    seething with intellectual intolerance, malice, and hatred.
He annihilated his political opponents, slaughtered thirty million
    people, appropriated their property, appropriated the entire ter-
    ritory the Czars had appropriated.
He was the greatest mass murderer in history, greater than Genghis Khan,
    greater than Hitler, greater than Mao,
Peerlessly the most cold-blooded conceited monster ever to impose his
    will and idea on the world.
So let his comrades worship his refrigerated corpse, while Schopenhauer
    snickers underground.

THE SYMBOL OF CHRIST

In my father's church, in the light of the stained glass window by
    the choir-loft
Christ was a living spirit casting his luminous love over the con-
    gregation,
His sympathy for each one of us, our special selves, very intimate
    and reassuring.
God was more abstract, a more impersonal force inside and outside
    the church, inside and outside our special selves;
Christ was a presence, God was a power, both absolutely benign,
    nothing to fear from either whether immanent or omnipotent,
Nor growing up from boyhood could I ever believe salvation from sin
    was the meaning of Christ, retribution the meaning of God,
Nor believe in the concept of original sin or a ludicrous last judge-
    ment or eternal punishment for whatever reason.
Biblical myths as parables have some significance, as compulsory
    beliefs they are an insult to the creative responsibility of
    any Creator.
But the spirit of Christ as the Son of God is symbolically true,
    for we all are the daughters and sons of God, all potentially
    divine.
Our birth is a miracle, our life is a miracle, our mind is a miracle
    of miracles, and Christ's compassion, do unto others, controls
    the mind.

A CHURCH OF ETHICS AND BEAUTY

Rationalize religion, 'tis the sense of beauty that stirs the soul
   to seek haven or heaven.
From kiva to temple to mosque and cathedral the lure is a place of
   perfection, a happy hunting ground, a glorious kingdom of God,
   an immortal extension of life.
Take the trail of beauty to the house made of dawn, house made of
   evening light,
Follow the path of righteousness to the higher harmonies of belief
   and well-being.
Rationalize religion, discard dissonant superstitions, doctrines,
   dogmas,
Build a church of ethics and beauty that every mind can subscribe to
   based on compatible essences.
Nay, compatibility is the snag---the unacceptable line of demarcation
   between what is beautiful, what is ugly, what is good, what is evil,
The dialectical confusion that makes a Tower of Babel out of every
   sociological structure no matter how solid the foundation and lofty
   the purpose.
Permanent values do exist regardless of esthetic and ethical rela-
   tivity;
Egyptian love poems written four thousand years ago stay true today,
   and Egyptian sculpture transcends the credulities and absurdities
   of Egyptian religion.
Reverence for the mystery and wondrousness of life is eternal, morality
   derives from constant correlations.

PRAYER

When a loved one suffers, our dread of doom
Tightens every nerve of our body like a barbed wire stretcher
Too tense to think clearly or eat sensibly, we sicken with fear
And pray in our hearts for the mercy of God.
Spare this loved one, spare everyone's loved one;
We know supernatural intercession is impossible, we pray nevertheless
Do me this personal favor, God, save this special one I love.
It concretizes our courage to appeal to an abstract omnipotence,
        to call it by a familiar name,
As when a quail pursued by a Cooper hawk flew straight to me as if I
        were God
And I flapped my arms, scared off the hawk, felt I had saved a soul.
But the hawk went hungry, perhaps it had little nestlings needing
        food, perhaps I had deprived them.
We can't compromise the cruelties, inconsistencies, brutalities of
        life with our anthropocentric concept of God.
To whom does the sheep- or lamb-to-be-slaughtered pray before the
        rapacious human stomach devours it?
We pray for spiritual salvation despite our animal appetites, we pray
        for this beloved one, we pray for that forlorn one,
Grant us Thy mercy, dear God!

THE RINGING STONES

The cliff was pale buff and pale pink feldspar trachyte
Typical turquoise matrix
Void of blue but down by the river
Black basaltic bellstones
Clinked underfoot with a silvershell sound.

Thin curved slabs a few prong-tapered
Each with that shy silver tinkle.
Strike two together they ring sharp staccato.
Set them in rows xylophonic
Hammer wild music up from the ground.

BUFFALO DANCE AT COCHITÍ

For fifty years have we seen the animal dances at the various
pueblos,
Ildefonso, Santa Clara, Santa Ana, San Felipe, Domingo, Jemez,
Taos, Tortugas
But never such perfection as the Buffalo Dance at Cochití that
clear warm Christmas morning.
It was the young Buffalo Mother who focalized and inspired it,
exquisite grace in every movement of her lithe slender body,
carved consecration on her beautiful Indian face.
The rhythm of her footsteps seemed a separate song over the drum-
beat, sometimes one foot suspended gliding back and forth, the
other pulsing up and down, alternating, a most subtle synco-
pation,
A superb arm gesture, right hand upraised majestic, swooping down
like a rush of rain, pulling up like growing corn, symbol of
fertility.
She drew the dance pattern around her like the design of an old
Cochití waterjar, the two buffalo-headed male dancers diago-
nalled away from her, circled back, the little antelope dancers
with stiff stick forelegs aligned horn-headed toward her.
She drew the landscape around her, the river valley, the cliffcave
canyons, tent rocks, pines, junipers, manzanita, dalea, ephedra,
Forgotten meanings reanimated in the dance, hovering over it almost
tangible.

MEDICINE SONG

Earth, sky, fresh air, wood and water sing to,
Identity, selfhood, soul-search cling to.
Sight lost at night
Day brings back bright,
Each reaffirmed fact
Words hold intact.
Inferences set in medicine song
Retain reality steady and strong.

HERE COME THE SINGERS

MATACHINA WITH BEAR DANCER

Parody of the pompousness of the White Man's religion,
Carefully avoiding ridicule of the White Man's God,
Distinguishes the Matachina Dance at Domingo.
The Queres Indians are master of burlesque,
They caricature Navajo and Hopi, Spanish and Gringo customs astutely,
Always with respect for what they make fun of.
An old Negro mammy they affectionately exaggerate,
Dressing a man with pillowed bosom and clashing colors,
Blacking his face, bandanna for a headdress, long white gloves,
Mimicking the soft Southern drawl "Howya doin', honey?"
But the Matachina Dance is serious satire,
A take-off on the legend of Montezuma's daughter marrying a White Man
Thereby uniting the Indian and White races, so to speak, or so to
        pantomime.
The liaison between the Conquistador Cortés and his mistress Malintzin
Is the source of the legend, very much mixed up,
Malintzin, Marina becoming Montezuma's daughter,
The epithet Matachina another agglomeration.
Often a local Virgin replaces Montezuma's daughter,
Usually a ten-year-old child, to be sure she's pure,
Dressed in white with a white wedding veil, a disgusting atrocity.
The Domingo dance is definitely symbolic---
Two long lines of men garbed in ecclesiastical costumes,
Black robes, purple palliums, visor-like masks, miter-like hats,
Face each other in opposite identical rows
And dance side by side like puppets in one position,
Jaunty jouncy steps swinging one leg across the other.
They form a corridor of the dusty danceground between them
And up the corridor come a man and woman, bridegroom and bride.
He is dressed like a high priest or royal potentate of some sort,
She wears a simple squawdress, bare-legged, bare-footed,
A flat spray of parrot feathers fastened atop her dark loose hair.
They dance side by side, he with those same stiff jaunty jouncy steps,
She with furious energy, trotting tangent, a strong knee-lift tread,
Crouching like a cave-woman, swirling against an enemy behind her,
Prancing back beside her partner, hopping two-footed to match his
        stiffness.

22

Her Indianness makes a fuddy-duddy of him, a church-trained puppet
    pulled by a set of strings,
But as they proceed to the canopied bench at the end of the corridor
He puts a little more fervor into it, as if trying to match her muliebrity.
They sit side by side on the bench like king and queen on a throne,
The chorus behind them chanting one phrase over and over and over
Yo no sé, yo no sé, yo no sé, yo no sé,
Indians obedient to the holy Spanish prescription
Don't think for yourselves, let us think for you,
You don't know anything about religion,
Just submit to the infallible authority of the Church.
Yo no sé, yo no sé, yo no sé, yo no sé.
Suddenly the beat of the drum sounds louder, faster,
The song shifts to Indian words vigorous, virile,
A mighty chorus of deep-throated male voices,
And from nowhere appears a lone Bear Dancer
Dressed realistic in a bear skin tied tight with an Indian sash.
He stomps up the corridor in a frenzy, raised a cloud of dust,
Spins around and around so fast he gets dizzy and falls down clownishly.
The onlookers laugh, the children giggle with delight,
The Bear Dancer get up, growls at them, roars at them,
Threatens them so ferociously they get scared and run.
Then he assumes a very dignified upright pose,
Walks like a man between the black-robed puppets
Who stand at rest impervious to his mockery.
He approaches the canopied bench where slant-eyed sit
The Indian woman and her White Man mate
And he shows off his full power before them, the Beargod no less,
Dances dithyrambic, leaps, lunges, spins like a whirlwind,
Disappears behind the singers in his own dust.

WINTER DEER DANCE

TURTLE DANCE — TAOS PUEBLO

PEACEFUL TRIBES AND PREDATORY TRIBES

Doves, turtle doves, mourning doves the most dove-like of doves
Fight as frantically as rufous hummingbirds, a malignant glare in
    their eyes.
All races and tribes of men fight over food or land or ideologies,
    kill kill kill, take take take, rule rule rule, rebel and rebel,
    raise Cain, raise hell.
Even the peaceful Pueblo tribes took captives and tortured them
    mercilessly, cut off their fingers while alive, made mummified
    finger necklaces sinew-strung in sets.
The most diabolical cruelty on record was committed at a glamorized
    pueblo I shall not name---
They captured one of our dragoon captains whose horse had been shot
    from under him and took him to the torture stake;
They slit his stomach open, pulled out the small end of his intestines,
    tied it to the stake, forced him to walk around and around the stake
    till all his intestines lay coiled in a heap.
I myself have seen a little Indian boy hold a little puppy on its
    back with with his knee, hold its eyes open with one hand, pour dust
    in them with the other.
It yelped piteously, almost human cries, while the older Indians looked
    on tolerant of torture,
But they would have grabbed me had I tried to stop the little fiend
    from blinding the poor little puppy,
And had I offered him ten dollars to buy the puppy it would have set
    a mercenary precedent for further fiendishness.
Treachery and torture were honorable traits among all Indian tribes
    whether peaceful or predatory.
How bravely does your victim withstand suffering? Make it a bit more
    excrutiating and maybe he'll whimper like a puppy.
It was not so honorable a trait among the Christian Torquemadas and
    Nazi genocidists and Communist annihilators
But quite as contemptible as Michael Angelo's painting of the Last
    Judgement.

NO WORD FOR ENEMY

From the Sierra to the sea it was a land of natural abundance,
Plenty for everybody, brodiaea bulbs, calochortus bulbs, wild onions,
    various roots, cattail shoots,
Hence they were called Digger Indians whether Miwok and Maidu or Yana
    and Yuki,
And above ground they gathered acorns, pine nuts, chia seeds, fruits,
    berries,
Shot tule elk and redwood elk with bow and arrow, ran down drift-caught
    winter deer on snowshoes,
Trapped fish in weirs, netted birds, lush country, plenty for everybody,
    no word for enemy.
But they would pluck bright feathers off a live bird to decorate their
    baskets,
The brightness stayed alive that way, you see, such a pretty quaint
    conceit.
They would snare a rabbit and bash its screaming head against a rock,
They would strangle a squirrel slowly while it squeaked and squealed,
They would pitfall a bear and poke it to death with sharp sticks and
    obsidian spears,
Plenty for everybody, no word for enemy.

REVENGE

Vestigial in North America today there is no such thing as a full-
blood Indian
And the more mixed their blood with Negro and White, the more mixed
their culture with Spanish and Anglo
The more they yammer about their Indian rights, especially their
rights to land they never owned in the first place.
They blame every White Man of the present generation for every con-
quest and iniquity of past generations,
Forgetting that tribe conquered tribe long before our acquisitive
ancestors arrived.
It was the Mongolian horde of Navajos and Apaches that drove the ab-
original Indians out of Mesa Verde and Chaco Canyon,
It was a band of Comanches that raided and burned the great pueblos
of Ojo Caliente and the Chama basin,
And had it not been for the support of Spanish Colonial settlers
and later Gringo dragoons, Taos and the Rio Grande pueblos would
have been completely destroyed.
But the young Taos Indian who worked for us would never believe Kit
Carson had saved his people from the enemy Navajos.
We were the enemy, we White people, we Ponsyna people, and the de-
risive way he intoned the word Pon-sý-na revealed the hatred in
his heart.
Superficially affable in order to keep a money-paying job, he re-
sented our having the money to give him a job,
He resented our very friendship, our efforts to help him and *his*
people retain their identity.
Revenge was his motive, Pan-Indianism his method, he wore a headband
around his loose-hung hair Apache style.
No doubt Pan-Indianism will be combined with the inchoate isms of
mestizo Chicanos and Muslim Negroes,
No doubt they'll manufacture time-bombs, atomic grenades, and try to
blow us Ponsyna people heeleewawa.

UFER'S CREDO

He was seldom sober during his terminal years, seldom took a bath,
    seldom changed his clothes,
Wore the same pinched-in peaked doughboy hat, dirty open-collared
    shirt, dirty doughboy breeches, scuffed leather puttees like the
    annealed buckskin costume of oldtime Rocky Mountain trappers.
As a disinfectant, alcohol probably pickled him 100% proof against
    dire diseases, but his snag teeth rotted in his head and his once
    burly body was flabby and floppy.
Too abulic to paint a picture he kept his ideas and ideals of art
    in a separate container from his whisky flask, rarely resorted
    to it.
At a group discussion on the principles of modern and classic art at
    the Taos Forum, however, his adrenalin glands became uncorked and
    he jumped to his feet stomping side to side.
"You bastards don't know what you're talking about! I'm Walter Ufer,
    you listen to me! I know every goddam theory of art propounded
    from Giotto's day till day after tomorrow,
I know how to draw, I know how to paint, and I paint what I feel, I
    paint what I see without trying to twist it into any goddam formula.
When I have a brush in my hand I am a pure man responding to the pure
    beauty of God's world, and that's more than any of you goddam bull-
    manure sons-a-bitches ever will be!
I'm Walter Ufer, you listen to me! I paint what I feel, I paint what
    I see!"

BIG SHELL MAN

The iridescent abalone shell, the big shell brought from the Coast
      by early Indian traders,
Symbol of great water, sea water, sky water, a fragment of the rain-
      bow held in hand,
Gave name to the main kiva on the north, and its chief was called
      Big Shell Man.
He was well qualified to be chief, a natural leader, powerful physique,
      powerful mind.
He wore his blanket toga-like, wore his hair in neat-tied chonga,
      made his own moccasins of deerhide and elkhide,
Spoke quietly in the soft Tigua tongue, his eloquence so poetic the
      interpreter had to grope for the right words to render it into
      English.
His purpose was to hold his people together, to keep them to the
      Indian way of life,
And our friendship, he said, was like the wind between the willows
      and the pines, his people breathing the same spirit our people did.
      not perverse, he accepted the White Man's tractor and plough as a
      logical improvement on the digging stick,
Cut his alfalfa with a mowing machine, fed his cattle in winter with
      hauled hay.
Two beautiful daughters he had, and two sons as wide-shouldered and
      wide-minded as he was, well trained in tribal lore.
The daughters stayed at the Pueblo, the sons he sent to college to
      read the great books in which the White Man stored his thinking.
The older one mastered Herbert Spencer's synthetic philosophy, trans-
      lated the gist to his father, the evolutionary principles, the
      curious belief in higher and higher development.
Yes, a child develops into a man, but the White Man develops into a
      crazy child running around in big crazy cities.
Big Shell Man considered big cities the wrong way to live, questioned
      himself what was the right way, the real way.
Neither the White Man's religion nor the Indian religion satisfies
      the sense of reality.
El Señor Jesu Cristo, the Spanish son of God, could walk on water
      and bring the dead back to life; no real man could.

Pai-an-quet-ta-tól-la, the Indian Red Person who shone like the sun,
 could fly straight up in the sky like a copper-colored humming-
 bird; no real man could.
Big Shell Man walked on earth, his flights of fancy returned to earth
 like a luminous dream.
Hold on to your land, my sons, my daughters, hold on to your land,
 my people,
Go up in the mountains, make an Indian shrine, think your own thoughts,
 belong to yourself,
Live with the earth, live with the sky, hold the rainbow in your hand.

KOSHAIRÍ

Like grey ghosts, phantoms, ancestor spirits
Floating on fox-like feet as if invisible
The Koshairi move between the lines of the Corn Dancers,
Arms upraised invoking the rainclouds,
Arms pointed down where the rain should go,
Arms stretched forward fingertips sprinkling
Water on earth shrivelled dry,
And they cry the Koshairi cry,
Exhale and inhale strength from the sky.
All life together grows
Perpetuate all then
Call and recall then
Spirit to spirit flows.

AGE OLD RHYTHM

MANA AND MANITOU

The primitive concept of Mana is the root of all religions, the mys-
    terious force of existence giving man his existence;
An instrumental force, not malign, supplicate it and it gives strength
    by reflective consciousness, as the power of prayer is the respon-
    sive resolve to what is prayed for.
The Plains Indian concept of Manitou personalized it, hail the Great
    Spirit, the anthropomorphic deity, placate it, make offerings,
    pay priests to intercede in your behalf.
Manitou, Tipni, Wakanda, Orenda were at least concerned with the in-
    dividual soul, whereas the literary Greek gods didn't give a whoop
    for anything except their own silly adulteries.
The Indian gods were nearer the true Mana, animals are nearer, coyotes,
    wolves, antelopes, birds, they apprehend it in moments of stillness
    and wonder.
At Taos we heard the quail calling year after year in the cedars and
    sage, guarding their coveys against hawks and hunters, and we helped
    protect them, fed them in winter, built a shelter shed against
    blizzards.
Callipepla squamata, Scaled quail, Blue quail, Cottontops, drab little
    gallinaceous birds but congenial, like a clan of little people, and
    they accepted us as amicable bipeds, wingless but bright-feathered.
Cooper hawks, Prairie falcons, weasels, snakes attacked them, and the
    Northern shrike could slaughter an entire brood of little chicks in
    three minutes, the most rapacious bird in nature with the most
    hideous rasping cry and most deceptive sweet song.
Combined coveys of about a hundred in autumn would be reduced to about
    twenty the next spring when they paired off to raise new broods.
    One year we noted a pair that couldn't raise a brood, the female had
    a broken dangling leg that somehow prevented nesting or hatching.
She could hop one-footed, could even limp on her broken leg, could
    bend her retrorse knee to feed closer to the ground, but couldn't
    raise a family.
The male was a gallant mate. He would lead her to the cracked corn
    we scattered, scratch a peckable pile for her, stand guard on his
    special lookout rock, call to her reassuringly.
Then she'd take sips from the birdbath pool, never hop in for a flap-
    wing shower, preferring dustbaths, powdering and preening herself.

Content with their duality they seldom joined the united covey in
   winter, though they were not ostracized as abnormal pairs usually
   are.
We anxiously watched them for three years, then the fourth spring the
   male appeared alone, his limping lady probably caught by a Prairie
   falcon.
Motionless he would stand on his lookout rock, motionless and silent,
   never calling to his mate, knowing she was dead, just standing there
   forlorn as if inviting the Prairie falcon to come get him too.
It was too sad to watch. What went on in his little quail brain we
   didn't try to imagine, but he seemed to be reasoning about his
   fate, his quail consciousness communing with the quail Mana.
Verily in the beginning was the Word and the Word was with God and the
   Word *was* God;
But there are verbal equivalents in the whole realm of life, the modu-
   lations of thought in a marmot's eyes seeing you meant no harm.
They all seek the reciprocal power of their Mana to reenforce their
   identity, and with man it is a continual test and re-test of truth
   in quest of reality,
The roundness of the world supersedes the flatness of the world, the
   spaceship on the moon supersedes the myths about the moon,
Mana the source of soul resonating throughout infinity and eternity.

BROTHER LEO

It was a tangible microcosm set on a sculpture stand so that you could
    look down on it,
A diaphanous fish carved in diaphanous selenite, swimming in the same
    element it was composed of.
Beside me a gaunt fellow was looking at it as curious as I was, his
    overwashed wrinkled white shirt, shiny mauve housejacket, dusty
    mauve trousers indicating he was very poor.
"It's a masterpiece!" I remarked. "Who did it, do you know?"
"I did," he replied with a shy indrawn smile, "and I wonder how I did."
"It's perfect!" I raved. "Put a high price on it and you'll get it!"
"Thank you, my friend, but it isn't for sale, I did it just to do it.
    I cannot sell my handiwork. I'm Brother Leo."
Ah, the sin of pride extends to the pride of accomplishment, why not
    to the pride of pridelessness, the pride of humility, the pride
    of sanctity?
Nay, sanctity is absolute, his face almost as diaphanous as the sculp-
    ture in selenite, his soul swimming in its own element.

DR. BADÉ

There are three kinds of religions, said Dr. Badé quoting Dr. Bouquet,
  religions which affirm the world, religions which escape the world,
  religions which transform the world.
Dr. Badé himself affirmed, a robust encyclopedic mind, President of
  the Pacific School of Religion, ethnologist, naturalist, John Muir's
  biographer.
I envied his friendship with Muir and pumped him about the California
  of Muir's day, the poetic age, the pantheistic age, I called it.
"Muir was no pantheist," Dr. Badé refuted. "He was an expert shingle-
  maker, you know, in spite of his love of nature, and a very success-
  ful farmer.
I don't know what his religion was, and don't ask me to define religion,
  young man. We'd disagree on positive factors."
We might have agreed, however, that the prevalent religion today is
  communism, a negative retrogressive religion pulling civilization
  back to socialized slavery under the rule of omnipotent parasites,
And we might have agreed that the concepts of goodness and Godness are
  essential to any true religion, critical reason essential to divine
  belief.

NOT A SPARROW SHALL FALL

Not a sparrow shall fall, mosquito be swat,
Nor cat maul a mouse but therefore but what
The sad eyes of heaven look down on the spot
And weep for each death--- 'tis a lie, is it not?

Prayer cannot alter nature's cruel course
Nor perpetuate life beyond fate's final force;
Cry out for mercy, cry yourself hoarse
While angels and pixies play tag in the gorse.

MONKSHOOD

Royal blue monkshood like luxuriant larkspur dyed deeper, the whole
    plant beautiful, the tall graceful stem with tattery palmate
    leaves like the flutter of birdwings in arrested motion around it,
    always growing in wild wet woodsy places by a mountain stream, indigo
    indicator of shy saxifrage and ladyfern up a creviced cliff.
Antithesis the whole plant poisonous, put it to the tongue and taste
    the tingling sensation of sure death, these wild lovely woods
    reek with macabre menace,
Baneberry, dogbane, amanita, zygandea, veratrum, conium that killed
    Socrates, cicuta the deadliest of all, monkshood the most deceptive.
Beware the deep blue true blue simile, beware the cowl that covers seed
    and creed, beware the anagogic aconite.

CITY OF THE HOLY FAITH

Indian ruins underlie the centuried city of Santa Fe, the Royal City
    of the Holy Faith of Saint Francis of Assisi here in the Sangre
    de Cristo Mountains of New Mexico---
Pithouses, kivas, adobe walls, fetishes, arrowheads, spearheads, grind-
    ing stones, pottery,
Cruder artifacts beneath the Pueblo stratum, culture superimposed on
    culture, belief on belief, faith on faith.
Old Santa Fe, the skyswept city, mountains lifting the heart in the
    pine-plunged blue, juniper hills so close and clean and livable,
    elms and maples shading the quaint little streets,
Tawny plains dipping down to cliff-cave canyons, wilderness beckoning
    beyond and beyond, massive white clouds soaring in symphonic sunsets,
    storm clouds, wisp clouds, days of ineffable cerulean serenity,
The whole country pervaded with benevolent beauty like the incense of
    juniper firewood, cedar, sabina, the inhaling inspiring.
The early Fathers found it easy to establish their religion here, the
    Indians receptive to ministration, the Church a refuge from death
    and disaster,
And the spirit of Christ was compassionate and kind, a personal friend
    to Indian, Spaniard, sheepherder, storekeeper.
Salvation from adversity is more meaningful that salvation from sin,
    but the doctrines, dogmas, and rituals of the Church center on sin,
    on catharsis of soul through faith in God.
Profoundly meaningful in the symbolic sense, discipline concominant,
    belief essential, disbelief punishable,
Agnosticism a vanity of vanities leading nowhere in the desert of
    desolation, stay staunch!
Here at the foot of the Sangre de Cristo Mountains almost four hundred
    years ago they built the city of Santa Fe giving solace to human
    suffering and intrinsic hope of heaven.

40

TWO TREES TALKING TO EACH OTHER

Two douglas firs on a high hilltop silhouette against the sky
Bent forward toward each other as if talking to each other,
The wind nodding or shaking their heads.
Mary and Martha articulating their likenesses and disparities,
Newton and Einstein swinging their arms around like contrary branches
     on the centripetal trunk of truth,
Dialogues on the hilltop, symposiums in the forest.

BEYOND THE MOGOLLON RIM

BEYOND THE MOGOLLON RIM

canto i

Dane Baldwin was the first man to drive sheep down into the river
  valleys beyond the Mogollon Rim, which instigated another violent
  episode in the perpetual feud between cattlemen and sheepmen, public
  domain part of the dispute,
And when a notorious gang of outlaws attempted to make an annhilation
  of it, shot Dane's brother Paul Baldwin in the doorway of his pine-
  log cabin, riddled Paul's wife as she knelt beside his body, Dane
  vowed vengeance and took to the warpath.
His neighbor Jack Kincaid, whose mountain ranch flanked his to the
  north, joined him on the warpath after three of his Mexican herders
  were slaughtered along with a lot of sheep. Jack Kincaid was the
  best shot in the Territory.
They promptly eliminated the outlaw gang but decided the feud wasn't
  worth the cost, so they settled in the Salt River Valley and became
  highly respected citizens, their reputation as gun-toters adding
  glamour to the respect.
Dane was a born speculator and promoter. He invested his capital,
  largely inherited from his father Henry Baldwin, once the foremost
  wool merchant of Boston, in farm lands, business property, and
  copper mines, quickly amassed a fortune.
He established his own bank in Phoenix with a Yankee manager to keep
  it thrifty and solvent, built a red sandstone mansion on the Tempe
  mesa, helped build the Reverend Matthew Schiller's red sandstone
  church near the new college, helped build the college.
Jack bought a ranch south of Tempe with plenty of irrigation rights
  for intensive alfalfa farming and rotary pasturing. He raised high
  grade stock and sold high grade hay to sheepmen and cattlemen alike.
The old Indian canal system had been extended and ramified, and Dane
  planned upper contour canals for the future, bought townsite land
  for development.
He raised horses on his estate, Morgan horses, planted shade trees
  around the paddock, but kept most of his 160 acres to native growth,
  preferring palo verde and mesquite to palm or orange trees.
Both men loved the desert, the clouds, the evening lights on the moun-
  tains a mystic allure regardless of the heat. Keep the wasteland
  wasteland! But Dane had an obsession against cholla.

45

A man couldn't walk though the damned stuff, a horse couldn't, a cow
   couldn't, a sheep couldn't, a coyote couldn't, only verdins could
   build their nests in it, elf owls and thrashers impervious to it.
Jack Kincaid harbored the wild birds and wild animals, renowned for his
   knowledge of nature and his gentleness and kindliness. Yet he was
   the strongest man in the country as well as the best shot, his hand-
   some clean-cut features and steady dark eyes trusted by everybody.
Dane himself was strong enough to deal with his adversaries, taller
   than Jack, lean and sinewy, shrewd grey eyes, tough grooved cheeks,
   a slight burr to his lips twisting with sardonic humor.
The Reverend Matthew Schiller was his humorless counterpart and para-
   doxical parallel. Dane was the first man to drive sheep west of
   the Mogollon Rim. The Reverend Matthew was the first man to plant
   a citrus grove in the Salt River Valley. With his own hands.
He had done much of the carpenter work on the church with his own
   hands, fitted the vault beams, installed the stained glass window
   to filter light on the choir loft.
For the stone work he had imported masons from Pennsylvania, wood-
   carvers from Michigan for the pews and pulpit, a beautiful church
   inside and out, a little Gothic cathedral in the middle of the
   desert, invitation, enter, rest, and pray.
Despite his Pennsylvania Dutch ancestry he was neither Lutheran nor
   Mennonite, and though he had been ordained a Methodist minister
   his creed was non-denominational.
God's grace must be earned, not endowed, and a work-ethic keeps the
   human instincts out of mischief, his metaphysical attitude very
   broad, his moral code very strict.
He took no salary for his services to the church, he was entirely
   self-supporting. Like Dane he had inherited a sizeable nestegg and
   added to it planting huge orchards, selling them at huge profit.
But the profits were dedicated to the church and good works. He said
   Dane Baldwin served Mammon rather than the Lord, which didn't pre-
   vent him from accepting Dane's contributions to the Lord.
He was absolutely humorless, his bland blue eyes owlishly abstract,
   his Moses beard indicative of his authoritative leadership of all
   wanderers in the wilderness.
Dane and Jack thought his sermons were scholastic but doggone dull,
   and the only reason they attended church was that he had two
   beautiful daughters who sang with the choir. He had sent them to a
   music college in Philadelphia.
He himself was a master musician. He could play any instrument, had
   composed cantatas and violin rhapsodies. The organ and piano were

his private indulgence, music his real religion.

The elder daughter Laura had a silvery lyric soprano which infatuated
Dane with it and her. He was too much older than she, besides being
tainted by divorce, to declare his infatuation.

Jack was openly in love with the younger sister Ellen, likewise haunted
by her voice. It was mezzo with a richer resonance that Laura's high
soprano, and her personality was richer and sweeter than Laura's.

She responded to his love idealistically, his superlative physique and
gentle disposition her heart's desire, but she feared she would be
an inadequate ranchwife, he was such a prodigious worker.

A sheepman. Wool, mutton, roast lamb. Jesus the shepherd of the human
flock no doubt ate roast lamb. Jesus the lamb of God sacrificed as
the savior of humanity. The absurdity of anthropocentric analogies.

Jack Kincaid had compassion for all forms of life, whether a crippled
kit fox, wounded broken-winged eagle, or an impoverished Mexican
family, gave refuge to them.

The Reverend Matthew admired his colossal strength and kindly char-
acter but forbade Ellen to marry him. He had been a man-killer,
had Jack Kincaid. She should marry his assistant pastor Jerome
Guthrie.

Actually Guthrie was his vicar, a substitute preacher whose eloquence
attracted and impressed large audiences. He quoted Shakespeare
and Browning, dispensed poetic parables like colored sticks of
candy, prayed with fanatic fervor.

Moreover he had an impressive stature, if overweight and flabby, and
a marvelous baritone singing voice, his duets with Ellen's mezzo
an operatic inducement for the Reverend Matthew's parishioners.

Your duty is to the church, my daughter. I have no sons; you are far
better qualified to carry on my work than Laura is. Just remember
Jack Kincaid is a dangerous killer whereas Jerome Guthrie is a con-
secrated Christian.

So Ellen married the hypocritical son-of-a-bitch.

canto ii

To build a dam on the Salt River, another on the Gila River, and con-
vert the fertile triangle between the junction of the two rivers
into a subtropical paradise was Dane's promotive dream.
He foresaw Phoenix would someday be the capital of Arizona, winter
capital of the West, date palms, orange groves, grapefruit groves,
all-year farming, inexhaustible mining, copper, silver, gold.
He cynically foresaw the attainment of his dream would drive him away
from it, the smear of civilization, but the surrounding desert was
vast enough to absorb it, the demotive dream a counterfoil to the
promotive.
Jack and he took many explorative trips horseback in the desert and
foothills, enterprise trips horse and buggy in the irrigable valley
lands.
Dane's buggy horse was a glossy black Morgan named Prince. He pulled
the shade-topped shade-tasselled box carriage a brisk pace over the
main roads, an aggrieved but determined pace over sandy side roads.
Starting early one hot morning in July the men were puzzled to see
Laura Schiller walking ahead of them down the road beyond her
father's stone church.
Her straight-backed figure and the sure-footed way she walked were un-
mistakeable, her neat grey twilled skirt and white shirtwaist in
trim accord, and her lilac-colored parasol!
"Going to Ellen's house," Jack observed worriedly. "Ellen's expecting,
you know."
"Yes, I know, and I can't understand why she ever let her father per-
suade her to marry a potbellied skunk like Jerome Guthrie."
"He has the gift of gab, Dane. I don't. And the ladies fall for that
sugar-coated baritone of his. I tried to tell Ellen he's the kind
of toady who turns into a bully. She said I had no right to call
him a toady."
"I'll bet she's found him out now, Jack. I'll bet she leaves him after
the baby is born. They aren't compatible. Mark my words, Jack, I
predict she will divorce him as my wife divorced me, though I con-
sider myself a darn sight better man than he is."
"I sure hope she does leave him, Dane."
Both men tipped their hats as they passed Laura. Her blue eyes flashed
recognition, sapphire blue eyes, gold blond hair. She half raised
her hand in a gesture of appeal, dropped it with a little wave of
dismissal.

48

They drove on slowly, the gesture sticking in their minds, conflicting
their mutual thought it's none of your business, there's nothing you
can do.

"Let's go back, Dane. Laura was asking for help. We should have
stopped then and there."

Dane gave a twitch to the left rein. Prince sensed an emergency, swung
the buggy around, set off at a faster pace, and they reached the
side road to Ellen's house almost at a gallop.

Nearing the house they saw an incredible flurry of lilac-colored parasol
and white shirtsleeve---the prim dignified Laura Schiller prodding
Jerome Guthrie with the parasol folded like a javelin!

When he protested she whacked him on the side of the head, poked him
in the rump, literally pushed him toward a neighbor's house.

It was too much for his Christian forbearance. He turned on her, grabbed
her by both wrists, forced her down to her knees, loomed over her.

Dane and Jack leaped out of the buggy, Prince ploughed four feet to a
standstill. Jack held back, fearing his own strength if he ever
layed hands on Jerome Guthrie. Dane pounced on him, spun him around
by the shoulder.

One blow to the guts, three to the face, and Guthrie fell backwards
on the hot sand, lay inert. Dane helped Laura to her feet, put a
bracing arm around her very gently.

"Are you all right, my dear?"

"Yes, I'm all right but he nearly broke my wrists. Thank heaven you
came back! He was going to crush me to death. I saw it in his eyes."

"What happened, Laura?"

"Oh, I begged him to go get Dr. Scott and he said only God could save
Ellen. He wouldn't go to the Nelsons for help, wouldn't budge, just
stood there praying a flowery prayer.

It infuriated me. I hit him on the head with the water pitcher. It
stunned him and I pushed him out the door telling him to go get
help or I'd kill him.

Ellen's in terrible shape, Mr. Baldwin. Please help me with her. Mr.
Kincaid, I know you love Ellen and she loves you. Please get Dr.
Scott as quickly as you can."

"Wherever he is, I'll get him," Jack promised running to the buggy.
Prince responded like a racehorse.

The air in the bedroom was stifling. Laura put a wet towel on Ellen's
forehead, a wet sheet over her twisted nightgown.

Dane improvised a cooling system of wet sheets over the open windows,
channelled a draft through the house from the screened kitchen porch.

49

Ellen was moaning and tossing feebly, too exhausted to keep trying to thrust the fetus out of her swollen tortured body, her beautiful face agonized.

"Did you suspect something was wrong when you started to come this morning?" Dane asked Laura.

"Oh yes. I should have gone for Dr. Scott yesterday. She was acting so furtive, so ashamed of her condition. I was afraid she might do away with herself."

Ellen stretched a groping hand toward their voices. Dane took it, held it with soothing firmness. She opened her eyes, grey-blue ocean deep eyes so different from Laura's searchlight sapphire.

"Mr. Baldwin!" she cried ecstatically, as if his very presence would get her well, Dane Baldwin the rich reliable banker, the community leader, Jack's best friend.

"Tell Jack," she gasped, "tell Jack it was an atrocious mistake---tell Jack I love him and only him---tell Jack we were meant for each other---tell Jack---tell Jack------."

A spasm of pain throttled her unconscious, and she was still unconscious when Dr. Scott hurried in. He was a short-statured, brawny-armed Scotsman, Hugo Scott, physician, surgeon, family psychologist.

He instantly saw Ellen's chances were very dim, the baby probably already dead, get it out and hope for a miracle. He asked Laura to heat a kettle of water.

"There's a coal oil stove on the kitchen porch, Doctor. I put a kettle to boil quite awhile ago."

"Good! Bring it in. You have basins, I see. Dane, break it easy to Jack Kincaid, will you. He's tense as a caged lion. Miss Laura and I can manage here."

Dane found Jack standing bareheaded beside Prince in the shade of a row of cottonwoods along the irrigation ditch, his dark eyes hard and bright as obsidian, ready for action.

"What became of Jerome Guthrie?"

"Sneaked off while I was fetching Doc Scott. How is Ellen?"

"She's mighty sick, Jack, but she gave me a nice message for you. She told me to tell you that it was an atrocious mistake, that she loved you and only you, that you and she were meant for each other. That's all."

"That's enough. Thanks, Dane."

"You had better fetch her mother, Jack. Ellen needs her and Laura needs her. I'll stay here on tap. If the Reverend Matthew interferes, tell him to go to hell."

The Reverend Matthew did interfere saying Ellen was Jerome Guthrie's
    wife, not Jack's and they would abide by his orders.
"Listen, Reverend, Jerome Guthrie sneaked off like the craven coward
    he is. Ellen needs her mother. I'm taking her. I advise you not
    to try to stop me."
"No, you can't stop us, Matthew," said Rebecca Schiller stoutly climb-
    ing in the buggy, grim determination superseding her usual docility, and
    Prince swirled.
She poured out her trepidations to Jack, trusting him as everybody
    did, her sweet face an older version of Ellen's, her spirit as
    generous and wholesome and earnest.
"I have no doubt it's a miscarriage, Mr. Kincaid. I had four myself,
    and I think Ellen took an abortion medicine. She didn't want Jerome
    Guthrie's baby. She was desperate.
In fact I saw her talking with Susy She-Wolf, the Papago medicine woman,
    you know. They say she can really get rid of an unwanted foetus.
    Every woman feels that way at times."
"I suppose they do, I don't blame them," said Jack sympathetically.
    "But abortion is risky, isn't it?"
"Very. Is your own mother living, Mr. Kincaid?"
"No. She died my second year in college. That's why I came West."
"Ellen said you told her nothing about your family except that your
    father was a steamboat captain on the Mississippi."
"Yes. He knew Mark Twain. I was born in St. Louis, Mrs. Schiller.
    My mother was a schoolteacher. She taught at a girl's seminary
    connected with Washington University."
"What did she teach?"
"Latin."
"Was she dark or fair?"
"Fair. Anglo-Saxon stock. My father was the dark one. Cornwall.
    King Arthur's country. He was a great reader. So was Mother."
"So are you, I take it. Jerome Guthrie pretends to be but he can't
    think for himself. Ellen never should have married him. He's
    nothing but an itinerant stump-thumper."
"He's more than that, Mrs. Schiller, or Ellen wouldn't have married
    him. But he's using the ministry for personal advance. He wants
    to be a star preacher, he wants fame."
"Quite true, Mr. Kincaid. Matthew doesn't see through him. Matthew
    is very gullible. Here we are. Ellen's house. It's pretty, isn't
    it. Matthew designed it."
A shade roof, architecturally synchronized above the gable roof and
    extended to porticoes at the sides made it look cool and comfortable,

51

and compared to a single-roof house it was.

The Reverend Matthew had given it as a wedding present to Ellen and Jerome Guthrie. Jack couldn't see anything pretty about it.

Dane assisted Rebecca's stoutness down from the buggy, nodded agreement it was a hot day, escorted her into Ellen's room. Dr. Scott had professionally cleaned up Ellen's body, smoothed the death grimace from her face.

"Ach, nein!" her mother cried, and Dane eased her onto a chair.

"Dr. Scott did everything he could, Mother," Laura said flatly, whiter-faced than the corpse. "It was too late."

"Ja! It was too late! My little Ellen! Tot! Tot! I couldn't prevent it, Herr Doktor. I wanted to send her back to my people in Pennsylvania. Matthew is so obstinate."

"Just be proud that you raised two beautiful daughters, Mother Schiller. Wonderful daughters. Laura is the most capable nurse who has ever helped me. You must rely on her from now on."

"I *am* proud! Two wonderful daughters, each so different, equally good. I keep them together in my heart, Herr Doktor. Forever."

"A cup of tea, Mother?"

"Ja! A cup of tea. Coffee takes too long to brew."

"I can brew the tea," Dane offered. "I'm a regular tea-toper, you know. Laura, I don't think I could face Jack again. Would you mind going out and telling him?"

"Certainly! I know he won't come in."

She found him standing bareheaded the way Dane had, rigid, cataleptic. She put a consoling sisterly hand on his arm.

It was like a shock. She felt the current of his strength flow into her, the slightest contact with that powerful physique a vitalizing force.

"She's gone, Jack."

He flinched. The dark eyes glittered at her.

"Did the baby survive?"

"Stillborn."

"I'm glad of that, Laura. It wipes the slate clean. She's mine now."

"She was always yours, Jack."

canto iii

Jerome Guthrie was hiding in the grapefruit grove when Jack came for
    Ellen's mother. He waited till the Reverend Matthew was alone to
    accost him and tell his side of the story.
He said Ellen had betrayed him by taking some kind of poison and he
    knew there was no hope for her except through prayer, but Laura
    came in and hit him with a pitcher and forced him outside to go
    for help.
She kept stabbing him in the back with her sharp-pointed umbrella and
    when he tried to wrest it away from her Dane Baldwin attacked him
    from behind, knocked him down.
They left him prostrate in the blazing sun and he would have suffered
    a stroke and died had not he revived sufficiently to crawl away on
    hands and knees.
"I can't believe Ellen would take poison," pronounced the magesterial
    lips in the Moses Beard. "Dane Baldwin would never attack anybody
    from behind. He smote you in the face, It's still bloody.
Come in the house and wash up, Jerome. I shall reserve judgment till
    I hear how Ellen is. Meanwhile you had better stay at the Tempe
    Hotel. Dane Baldwin and Jack Kincaid are violent men."
"Yes sir, I think that would be wise. I can't cope with them in my
    present predicament. I shall continue to pray God to spare Ellen's
    life."
Laura's version of the story was scathing, Jerome Guthrie safely en-
    sconced at the hotel. She accused him of being a sanctimonious fraud,
    refusing to go for help, refusing even to give Ellen a drink of water.
"All he did was stand there and pray. Pretty little prayers, literary
    prayers. He's not a man, he's a nauseating toad."
"You are maligning him, Laura. He came here and confessed to me. He
    told me he dared not leave Ellen's bedside lest she fall out and
    injure the baby. He knew only God could save her."
"God didn't save her. Dr. Scott didn't save her. Dane Baldwin didn't
    save her. I didn't save her. She's dead. Do you understand me?   53
    My sweet beautiful sister Ellen is dead."
"Tot!" moaned Rebecca. "Ja, we have lost her, Matthew. She was sick
    from the beginning. We should have sent her back to my people in
    Philadelphia."
He couldn't absorb it, his eyes blank, dazed. But a minister of the
    Lord has to say something, has to mumble platitudes.

"It's a terrible blow for me, Laura. I pray she died peacefully. I
pray for God's mercy in this hour of trial and tribulation."
"If you talk like that I'll scream!" shrieked Laura. "She didn't die
peacefully! She died in agony! It's all your fault. You made her
marry that monster. You killed her!"
"Laura, go to your room and reconsider what you have said. You are
hysterical. I shall expect your apology in the morning."
"Oh no you won't! I'm leaving this house this minute. Dr. Scott said
he would like to train me for his office nurse. I'll do anything
to escape your self-righteous tyranny."
He strode at her to shake her, to punish her, but she eluded his grasp,
ran out, her mother calling after her "Laura, don't leave me, don't
leave me!"
"I won't go far, Mother," she called back. "He'll be more considerate
of you if he has only one female to do his bidding."
Cumulus clouds colored the late afternoon sunlight, the desert enchanted.
Ellen up there. Her lovely mezzo singing in the sky. No blemish on
her soul. Pure as pure.
Dr. Scott's house was in town. Laura knew his wife would welcome her
right in. Dane Baldwin's house was a mile northeast. She walked
northeast.
Such spacious grounds! Arizona cypress lined the driveway, the red
sandstone mansion with its thick walls, tile roof, and wide eaves a
staunch sanctuary against Arizona heat and mirages of the mind.
The stables and paddock for the Morgan horses were set in a grove of
cottonwoods. Prince was there, so Dane was home.
He had built the house for his wife Mercedes, a Vassar graduate who
couldn't stand the dry climate and crude culture of Arizona. One
of the Boston Lowells, Mercedes Lowell. She returned to the land
of baked beans and codfish and Cabots.
A congenial unservile Welsh couple, George and Beulah Evans, took care
of the horses and house and Dane. They were his family.
Laura clacked the iron knocker on the heavy oak door. Beulah opened
it, astonished to see the minister's fastidious daughter sagging
there, hatless and dishevelled.

54 "Good heavens, Miss Laura, you look faint! Sit here on the bench and
I'll bring you a cup of tea."
"No tea, thank you, Mrs. Evans. I'm quite all right. I presume Mr.
Baldwin told you my sister Ellen died in childbirth."
"Yes he did and he's awfully upset about it. So is Mr. Kincaid but
he didn't say a word. He breaks my heart, Miss Laura. He's locked
it all up inside himself."

"Is he still here?"

"No, he rode away on his saddle horse like a lone Indian. Mr. Baldwin is in the library. Do you want to see him?"

"Yes. Please show me the way."

Beulah led her to the library and Laura walked in unannounced. Dane was at his desk writing an advisory note to Matthew Schiller in regard to Jerome Guthrie.

"My dear girl, what now? I hope it isn't more bad news."

"I have left home, Mr. Baldwin. I quarrelled with my father. He killed Ellen. He compelled her to marry that hideous monster. I hate him. I've come to you because--------"

"Go on, my dear. Don't be embarrassed. Get it off your chest. If I can help you in any way you can count on me to the limit."

"The limit is rather extreme, Mr. Baldwin. I have watched you watching me while I sat in the choir loft and I think you love me. I saw it in your eyes. I know you are twenty years older than I am but I should like---I mean I---"

"Whoa! Hold your horses, young lady! Let *me* do the proposing! Hell's bells, Laura Schiller, I have been in love with you ever since I first heard you sing!

You were the golden girl with the silver voice to me, you inspired me, lifted me right out through the stained glass window. I adore you! Therefore I ask you, will you marry me, Miss Laura ma'am?"

"I will, kind sir, and you will find me a faithful wife. But I warn you I have many faults. I'm selfish, I'm acquisitive, and very very practical, though not cold-blooded, I hope."

"I'll settle for whatever you are, Laura Schiller. You couldn't be so selfish as my first wife. It was a great relief when she left me and wangled a divorce. Her memory will never come between us, my darling."

The wonderful feeling of his arms around her, the wonderful feeling of male protectiveness. Ellen deserved it and didn't get it. Take it, take it, be selfish, Ellen would want you to be.

She slept in the downstairs guestroom that night, Beulah lending her a nightgown and toothbrush, and the next day Dane took her to the Emporium for a complete new outfit of clothes.

They were married by a justice of the peace, their rapport without a single snag except they could not attend Ellen's funeral. Nor could Jack Kincaid.

George and Beulah Evans did, and Dr. Scott stuck at Rebecca Schiller's side like a vigilant son. The college chaplain conducted the services.

55

Telephones had recently been installed in the Phoenix-Tempe area, so Laura was able to keep in discreet touch with her mother. Reconciliation with her father was impossible.

"I don't think he feels a whit of remorse for Ellen's death. His obtuseness is impregnable. I'll never forgive him, never!"

"Well, the old saying that his good qualities outnumber his bad ones is quite true, Laura. He's a great man. He hasn't disowned you. He's being very magnanimous."

"I'll admit he's a great man. It makes his domination all the more insidious. It's the hold he has on Mother, yet he's absolutely dependent on her. They're yoked together like a team of oxen."

The Reverend Matthew had a quixotic streak of which Laura was unaware. He withdrew his account from Dane's bank and deposited it in a rival bank, not vindictively but to spare awkward contacts,

Then he payed Jerome Guthrie a lavish price for a quitclaim on Ellen's house, sold the house at a lesser price, deposited the money in Laura's name in the rival bank.

The owner of the bank was a friend of Dane's in spite of their competitiveness and jocosely informed Dane of the account. Dane kept quiet about it knowing Laura would never accept any sort of retribution from her father.

However it was common talk that the Reverend Matthew had given Guthrie a generous stipend to get out of the country and stay out. He obtained a new co-pastor through the Methodist board, an intelligent young man with an affable wife, William H. Conrad, D.D., Ph.D.

Laura felt deliciously emancipated. She loved the big house, the hand-carved furniture, the collections of Navajo rugs, Pueblo pottery, Indian baskets, and the ebony square piano in the parlor, which she preempted.

The library fascinated her. Books on every subject including one by Dane Baldwin on corporation law. History, science, fiction. Agriculture. Stock raising.

And they raised their own stock, their first child a boy, born in the downstairs guestroom where Laura herself had been introduced into the Baldwin household.

Dr. Scott said it was an easy delivery. Laura didn't dispute him. Dane carried the glad tidings to the Schillers in person.

Rebecca beamed, splattered German interjections amid her effusive English. The Reverend Matthew received Dane politely, approving his amicable overtures.

DESERT PEAKS

"We are going to name the boy Mark since the event marks a fuller life for Laura and me. It's a good Gospel name too, Reverend. It comes right after yours."

The bland blue eyes indulged in a glint of biblical amusement. He let Rebecca go with Dane in order to bring back a descriptive account of his grandson.

"He's the image of you, Matthew," she reported, by intuitional entelechy rather than actual observation. "Very serious-looking. Not a whimper out of him. They have asked Dr. Conrad to christen him."

Christening was Laura's condescension to Dane's diplomacy. She had renounced religion, detested it, but if Dane wished to bolster her father's affection for the boy, let him.

They named their second baby, born two years later, Rebecca. Becky Baldwin. A dainty child, straight-backed, well-formed, quite pretty.

"The papoose who swallowed her cradle board," Dane commented dryly, enraptured with her, the reddish hair, greenish eyes a throwback to some unknown ancestor.

Their third and final offspring, born after another two-year interval, they named Matthew. Matt. Which was ironical humor on Laura's part, for he was the image of Dane, the same slight burr on his lips, a joyful little grinner and kicker.

Becky was a little Laura, her greenish eyes intense green as she grew older, emerald against Laura's sapphire. And there was music in her. She listened avidly when Laura played the piano.

Having a family stirred Dane's ambition to Utopianize Arizona, get the irrigation dams built on the Salt and Gila rivers, ramify the canal system, expand the educational and cultural facilities.

His private speculations were solid enough but to protect Laura and the children in case something happened to him, to guard against financial adversity, such as the silver panic of 1893, he recorded his most valuable asset in Jack Kincaid's name.

It was the old Tektol silver mine near Casa Grande. He had bought it for a proverbial song. The main vein and parallel stringers had apparently petered out, the Tektol Company had abandoned it, and his bank held a mortgage on it.

58

Jack and he were more than textbook geologists. They were convinced that the vein continued at a lower level beyond a rubble-hidden fault slippage.

They prospected the shaft-ventilated adits and found small deposits of gold in side pockets, as in the Wickenburg mines, which further convinced them of Tektol's potentiality.

Tektol Mountain and forty thousand acres of wasteland went with the
    deal, and there was plenty of deep-well water in the canyon for
    steam-power stampmills and for leaching concentrates.
The railroad from California to Tucson and El Paso solved the long-
    distance hauling problem. Jack assured Dane he could sell out for
    millions someday.
"Don't worry about Laura and the kids. I'll take care of them if any-
    thing happens to you, Tektol or no Tektol."
Jack's experiment with rotary pasturing and cross-breeding of Rambouillet
    stock for an all-purpose Western range stock had been extraordinarily
    successful. He could take care of a regiment.
But Laura was disturbed, at first, by Jack's marriage to Fern McMurtry.
    It seemed an apostasy to his love for Ellen.
"Never say a thing like that about Jack Kincaid," Dane scolded her.
    "He's a mystic. Ellen is his immortal belovéd. He simply gave
    shelter to Fern as he would to a crippled animal."
Crippled was the word. Dane related how old Tom McMurtry had died
    leaving Fern and her little sister Heather practically destitute,
    a mortgage on the house which Dane cancelled.
Fern rented rooms to college students, taught grammar school in Tempe,
    worked herself to the bone, got sick. Dr. Scott suggested Jack
    should take her on as his housekeeper and feed her up.
Which he did, treating her and Heather as if they were his own sisters.
    Fern had an inheritable deformity, the third and fourth fingers of
    her right hand fused together, which prevented her from ever dream-
    ing of marriage.
So of course Jack legally married her to give the two orphans a good
    home for the rest of their lives. Laura became very fond of them,
    agreed that Jack had not committed an apostasy.

canto iv

Dane had come to the wild and woolly West largely because his father
    was a wool merchant and he wanted to see wool on the hoof.
The New Mexico mountains, the Plains of San Augustin, the Mogollon
    Plateau, the Tonto Basin obliterated Harvard and law school. Be
    a man. Be a rancher.
The feud made him be a banker, and as a banker he loaned money to sheep-
    men of the Mogollon grasslands and to Angora goat raisers, mohair
    as valuable a market as wool. Which tied up the bank assets con-
    siderably.
And he still had enemies. When he overinvested bank money in specu-
    lation deals they ganged up on him, organized a run on his bank,
    and he went bankrupt.
Jack Kincaid always kept his bank account minimal, reinvesting the
    profits from his ranch back into the ranch, so he wasn't hurt much
    by the collapse. He knew Dane wanted to play the game his own way
    but he stood ready to help if necessary.
Dane played the game shrewdly. To pay big and little depositers pro-
    portionately and avoid confiscatory claims he asked his old friend
    Judge Henderson to appoint a trustee to distribute what funds he
    could raise.
He immediately sold the stone mansion and 160 acres to a New York
    outfit for a golf club, sold his Mogollon ranch to a Texas cattle-
    man, his copper mine at Globe to a Bisbee corporation, his business
    properties for whatever he could get.
Judge Henderson gave him plenty of rope. "Dane Baldwin can pull rab-
    bits out of a silk hat, silk hats out of a rabbit's ears," he said.
The Tektol mine, not listed in his name, was a safe secret for eventual
    recoup. The Morgan horses he gave to Jack, and Jack gave the home-
    less Baldwin and Evans families refuge along with the horses.
There was an old Spanish hacienda on the ranch which Jack had restored
    to preserve as a historic landmark, two wings and a patio, rooms
    inset from the resolana portales like a hotel.
They kept the children out of school because of the general animosity
    against Dane, sparing them the innuendos and outright jeers due to
    their father's disgrace.
Mark was twelve, Becky ten, Matt eight. They diligently studied under
    Laura and Fern's instruction. Heather McMurtry attended grammar
    school in Tempe, Jack taking her and fetching her in the tassel-
    topped buggy, Prince like a racehorse.

She and Matt were the same age and were naturally attracted to each
    other, imaginative little playmates. Laura deliberately eavesdropped
    on their conversations and make-believe games.
"She's such a nice little girl, Dane. I can see why Jack adopted her.
    She's not so precocious as Becky but she's very intelligent, and
    such a lovable child, clean and sweet."
Clean clear brown eyes, smooth brown hair brushed back in a hank with
    a silver clasp at the nape, dainty young-girl neck, soft-bridged
    freckled nose, irresistible smile, Fern was sister, mother, and
    preceptress to her.
She had escaped the finger-fusion defect of the McMurtry chromosomes
    but Fern had instilled in her a premature dread of passing it on,
    the taboo you must never have children.
Not a morbid dread. Simply a matter of eugenics. There's only one
    Jack Kincaid in the world but if you ever meet a man remotely
    like him you can marry him.
Fern was happy enough. She was an older version of Heather, her brown
    eyes as clean and clear, her nose sharper, her bluish teeth squinched,
    her smile rather anxious. Dane said she reminded him of his brother
    Paul's valiant wife.
He decided it would be wise to settle his family in California until
    he could get a fair price for the Tektol mine, which might take
    years. He approached the Reverend Matthew for assistance and was
    overwhelmed by his willingness to finance the move.
"It's a good idea, my son. Where do you plan to settle?"
"Somewhere near Pomona College, Father Schiller, I want the children
    to have a thorough education. A couple of rental houses and a
    small orange grove would give Laura a steady income."
"Pomona is a Congregational college. I have no objection to the Con-
    gregational creed. It is neither Calvinist nor Augustinian. Yes,
    it's a good idea. Laura could manage an orange grove easily.
Perhaps you know that the money I retrieved from Ellen's house I have
    kept for Laura and the children. I shall make her a gift of it."
"She wouldn't accept it now, Father Schiller. She may later. If you
    will make me a loan of cash money I'll buy the property in Laura's
    name and pay you back as soon as I have cleared all my debts here."
"You don't intend to settle in California yourself?"
"No. I'll stay here and stick it out. Eventually I'll pay back every
    penny I owe, It's a requirement for regaining my self-respect,
    earning the grace of God, as you would say."

"That, my son, is the root of ethics. I have great confidence in your
business judgment. I don't think you were unscrupulous; you were
the victim of circumstances."

"I was the victim of my cautious cashier. He opposed my methods and
talked too much outside, which tipped off my enemies to take ad-
vantage of me at a weak moment."

The Evanses accompanied the Baldwins to California, the train through
Casa Grande taking them direct to Pomona. Dane bought two rental
"bungalows" in Claremont at the edge of the college campus and a
thirty-acre orange grove within walking distance of it.

The well-built frame house, painted yellow with green trim, had a
quaint turret at the west corner, an L-shaped veranda front and
east, the crescent driveway centered around a magnificent live
oak. The owners were moving to Seattle.

The caretaker's cottage was set in a clump of deodars at the cross-
roads. Dane and Laura deeded it with five acres to George and
Beulah Evans full title.

Laura was delighted with the place, the Evanses ecstatic. A cool grey
haze often swept in from the ocean fogs, the ocean not too far away.
The people were friendly but very Californiac, full of bigger and
betterness.

"Every professor thinks himself broader-minded than every other pro-
fessor," Dane complained.

He returned to Arizona and bought a neat little brick house near Casa
Grande replete with a windmill, bought a tough little buckskin
horse and pack-mule for prospecting trips to the Tektol mine,
by devious decoy routes.

The property had belonged to an old couple from North Dakota who never
wanted to see a North Dakota winter again. They had died there con-
tentedly, their children grown and supportive of their retreat.

The house had two bedrooms, an ornate old-fashioned parlor, and a shed-
roofed kitchen. Dane liked to batch, did his own cooking on a coal
oil stove, except when he splurged at the Chinese restaurant.

62 He converted the parlor into a library, the books he had stored at
Jack's ranch overfilling it, so he built shelves in the bedrooms.
He recorded the place in Jack's name, as he had the Tektol mine.

A Mormon handyman had helped the old couple build the house and it was
of typical Mormon architecture, gable roof with a drafty air-cooling
attic, the shed-roofed kitchen to the north, a dugout for milk, meat,
and vegetables near the kitchen door.

A pole and brush-covered ramada in the corral down the bank of the
   arroyo gave the little buckskin horse and a pack-mule ample shade
   all day long.
Laura and Becky, sometimes with Matt, payed Dane irregular week-end
   visits during the winter months, an overnight trip by train. In
   summer he payed conscientious visits to Claremont, a Papago Indian
   named Zeke Morning Star taking care of his precious little buckskin.
Mark was a confirmed Californiac, a serious boy, almost as humorless
   as the Reverend Matthew. He made good grades at high school, at-
   tended church solemnly, worked like a man in Laura's orange grove.
Laura attended church only to sing with the choir, her silver voice the
   main attraction at college sociables also, and she gave piano lessons
   to increase her income.
Becky was a prodigy pianist. Dane loved to watch as well as hear her
   play, the intense concentration of those green eyes, the calm mastery
   of her smooth brow, the exquisite profile, Laura's profile.
Matt was the scientist of the family, rock collector, butterfly netter,
   studying advanced books on geology and entomology, the slight burr
   on his lips tightening when resolved to get something or do something.
Yes, the change was good for the family, the incentives as thick as
   orange blossoms. But Dane doggoned the foggy grey climate and
   insipid Pomona professors.
"Oh, come now, Dane," Laura protested. "I've met some very interesting
   professors here and very talented hausfraus. They're just as smart
   as your old Harvard professors."
"Smarter. But hell's bells, Laura, all professors are intellectual
   imbeciles, or imbecile intellectuals, from William James on down.
   Your father's got more guts than any of them."

canto v

An agent from a Silver City outfit who knew the history of the defunct
Tektol Company and the probable significance of the fault slippage
approached Jack Kincaid sooner than Dane expected.

Jack was not a dickerer. Dane needed a million and a half to clear the
balance of his debts. That was the figure Jack set and that was the
figure Jack got.

Judge Henderson didn't question the money coming from Jack. He pro-
claimed Dane Baldwin a man of honor. Dane personally payed back the
loan he'd had from the Reverend Matthew and felt he was a free man
again.

Now he could join his family in California, start new enterprises,
build asphalt highways across the Yuma desert, dams on the Colorado
River, townsites around bluewater lakes.

Forget it! Stay right here in your little old brick house and be a
doggone hermit! Tickle Gila monsters under the chin, read all the
books you haven't read in your doggone library!

"I'm just a pooped-out tea-toper," he told Laura. "I ain't got no
ambition to amount to nothin no more nohow." She didn't try to
urge him. His visits to Claremont were companionable enough. He'd
had his day. Let the children have theirs.

Mark was making his mark all right, topnotch authority on orange pro-
duction, engaged to the daughter of the president of the fruit
grower's association.

Anthea Laclede. She had a rose-olive complexion, mottled ripe-olive
eyes, a sinuous sensuous body, and a possessive passionate dispo-
sition.

But she was loyal to Mark during the Kaiser's war. He enlisted, in-
fantry captain, won a distinguished service medal, returned intact,
married her, raised kids and avacadoes.

The war with his Vaterland jolted the Reverend Matthew. He had served
in the Civil War, which he called fratricide, and the killing of
German soldiers by American soldiers was patricide.

He retired from the ministry, sold his grapefruit grove, moved to Clare-
mont, experimented with apple and sweet cherry trees in a non-decid-
uous climate.

Laura was glad to have her mother nearby and for her sake moderated her
animosity toward her father, his gnarled hands and old-age decrepi-
tude stirring her compassion and daughterly sense of duty.

64

His Moses beard was nevertheless a symbol of male domination to her
    and she still held him to blame for the obscene horror of Ellen's
    death
The better aspects of his religious zeal, his musical genius, were
    reincarnated in Becky. She married the widowed minister of a pro-
    gressive church in San Francisco, his organist. It was a joyous
    marriage and they named their daughter Allegra.
Matt had very little of his grandfather's character in him. He was
    Dane's son, skeptical, sardonic, determined, the same limber physique,
    star athlete at Pomona, sprinter, broadjumper, football halfback.
He worked as hard as Mark and George Evans tending Laura's orange groves
    plural, contributed to her prosperity, and when she bought a Cadillac
    he was her chauffeur.
The trips to Arizona were more exploratory by car than by train. Matt
    was majoring in geology, aiming for a doctorate. "I can show you a
    thing or two about mineral deposits," Dane induced.
They prospected for theories instead of investments, Laura a game
    camper-outer, and always ended up with a visit to Jack Kincaid's
    ranch before looping back to California.
Matt's boyhood hero-worship of Jack Kincaid had matured into emulation
    of the man. Clean habits, a clean logical versatile mind, a tremen-
    dous worker. Nobody could emulate his physique.
His boyhood fondness for his playmate Heather McMurtry had also matured.
    History was her major at the State College, in preparation for a
    teaching career, botany her avocation.
She was not musical but very adept at scientific drawing and had helped
    illustrate a textbook on desert flora by her favorite professor Dr.
    Wallace. Matt admired it, admired her, shunned involvement.
She had grown prettier if rather reserved, her clear brown eyes intro-
    spectively resistant. She didn't dance, her social activities very
    restricted. Which suited Matt's wariness of women.
There had been only one sex incident between them as children, a cata-
    lytic image of Jack Kincaid standing naked on the bank of the ranch
    arroyo.
A flash flood had swept a Mexican boy into a backwash whirlpool where
    he clung to the branches of a tall palo verde, the main torrent a
    raging linear vortex.
Knowing his clothes might snag, Jack stripped and plunged in, tugged
    the boy safe to the bank, stood there getting his breath, his white
    body glistening like a Greek god's carved in marble.
The vision fascinated them, united them in a mystic feeling preter-
    naturally adult, scared them, they slunk away.

65

Fern's warning don't ever marry unless you meet a man like Jack Kincaid
persisted through Heather's adolescence and college encounters. She
didn't dance lest her affections become attached.

Matt didn't dance because he thought dancing a promiscuous indulgence
and silly waste of time. The Pomona co-eds gave him up as a hopeless
case. He was too untouchable an athlete, too cynical a student.

Grand Canyon changed their viewpoint literally and emotionally. Matt in-
vited Heather on a geological survey of the Colorado Plateau, plenty
of room in the Cadillac, Laura and Dane sitting on the back seat.

A day of swift spring clouds when they reached the rim, pinkish brown
clouds, nacreous white shifting the lights on the buttes and chasms,
geology temporarily tossed to the bottom of the abyss.

They left their chaperones at the hotel and hiked to a promontory, en-
thralled by the sublimity of it. They looked and looked at it,
looked in each other's eyes, suddenly were in each other's arms.

Too conspicuous on the rim they hurried to the privacy of a juniper
thicket, talked and talked as they had looked and looked, trying
to explain themselves to each other.

Her honesty made her drag in the inheritable finger-fusion as an ob-
stacle to marriage, hoping he would demolish it, which he did.

"Your sister Fern put that bugaboo in your noodle. Your fingers
aren't joined so what are you worrying about? It's a harmless
defect anyhow."

"Yes but our children will surely inherit it."

"Yes but my eye! It keeps Fern from playing the piano and that's a
bonanza. Becky can drive you crazy playing one phrase over and over
till she gets just the right nuance.

If you don't want children we won't have children but I want *you*,
Heather McMurtry, and by golly I'm going to have you whether you
have leprosy or whether I have hydrophobia!"

"Oh, Matt, I love you so much, so much, so *much!* I think we have always
loved each other. We didn't realize it when we were little and we're
almost afraid to realize it grown up!"

"Do you love me more better grown up than when I was little?"

"Most best, darling, much most best!"

They were still unable to talk rationally on their return to the hotel,
Laura and Dane suspiciously waiting for them.

"Hell's bells, Matt, where the devil have you been? Down the Bright
Angel Trail?"

"Up it, Dad, up it! Heather met a feller at the top and got engaged
to him."

66

"She did, did she? How is he going to support her on a doggone geology professor's salary?"

"He's quitting college day after tomorrow, Dad. He's going to follow in his father's footsteps and speculate in land deals right here in Arizona. Build houses. Good houses. Stone houses."

"You were born in a stone house, Son. Your grandfather built a stone church. You've got stones on the brain. Laura says you are too granite-minded to make a good husband."

"I haven't said a word," said Laura. "There is no one I would rather have for a daughter-in-law than you, Heather. I shall never dictate who shall marry whom."

CLOUDS AT SUNSET

Canto vi

The Reverend Matthew succeeded with his sweet cherry and Gravenstein
   apple experiment. He was eighty-six, worked in his orchard every
   day, walked to it the half mile from Laura's place.
She had insisted as infirmities beset him and her mother that they
   come live with her so that she could take care of them properly.
   She felt virtuous in offering her unforgivable father a home.
Dane never told her that it was her father who had loaned him the money
   to buy the very home in which she so attentively nursed their needs.
They didn't trouble her for long. Her intermediation deprived them of
   their sustaining dependence on each other. Rebecca died painlessly
   in her sleep, the forlorn Matthew a month later.
Laura and George Evans found his body lying under a jacaranda tree, his
   hoe set carefully beside him like an instrument of the Lord, his
   Moses beard pathetic in its quiescent dignity, his strong sensitive
   work-gnarled hands stretched over a silent keyboard. Laura wept.
"Who will remember him after you and I are gone?" she appealed to Dane.
   "Who will remember Ellen after Jack and ourselves are gone? It's a
   closed circle in two generations."
But the closed circle drew Laura and Dane closer together. They retro-
   spected all winter in the little brick house in Casa Grande around
   Matthew Schiller's ambivalent character and their own.
They agreed he should have been a composer instead of a minister, his
   motets and cantatas unique. A subtle sense of humor showed up in
   his inversion of phrases and surprise repetitions.
"He often said Beethoven was as pure as Christ," Laura recollected. "But
   he said the same thing of Hegel. He read Hegel in German, you know."
"Hell's bells, I couldn't read Hegel in Papago! I never could see what
   your father really believed in, Laura. He had a skeptical streak in
   him. He once confided to me that he was neither trinitarian nor uni-
   tarian. Meaningless distinction, isn't it!"
"Isn't it! Father, Son and Holy Ghost! Always a male deity, male
   messiah, male pervasiveness, the Virgin Mary immaculately impreg-
   nated by monstrous maleness! Ellen. I hate religion, any religion!
   I'm glad I married a gun-toter instead of a bible-toter."
"So am I, Miss Laura ma'am. But since you and I are both such incor-
   rigible heathens, can you tell me what we really believe in?"
"We've questioned that before. A sort of pragmatic ethics, I think.
   Father certainly believed in the Ten Commandments and we go on from
   there. You wrote a book on corporation law, you know."

69

"Yes, and the book I'm writing now goes a bit further. Religious and
    economic beliefs make legal beliefs and legal beliefs yield to your
    pragmatic ethics. Gun-toters made the history of Arizona. I'll
    probably be shot at sunrise for saying so in my book."
"No you won't. Hurry up and finish it. Nobody is better qualified
    than you to write a history of Arizona.
"Just so you don't call it *an* history. It's almost finished. Heather
    said she would type it for me.
"She's a jewel, our Heather. What was *her* father like, Dane?"
"Old Tom McMurtry? He was a dreamer like me. He kept a hardware store
    in order to deal with something tangible. I dealt in land and solid
    rocks."
"How did he lose his money?"
"Trusted his bookkeeper too completely. The man absconded. It ruined
    him. He wouldn't prosecute."
"And left his daughters penniless! Thank heaven you and Jack saved
    them! Fern would have died."
"Undoubtedly. Not Heather. She has better health and more talent.
    Matt sells those houses as fast as he builds them because of her
    designs. They make a swell team."
Borrowing from the Phoenix bank to get started had been easy for Matt
    with Dane's redeemed reputation behind him. But he was a go-getter
    anyhow, a sprinter, a winner.
He and Heather tried to persuade Dane to live with them in their air-
    conditioned house, and if he liked Chinese cooking they would get
    a Chinese cook for him.
"I'm staying in my lil ole brick house till I finish my book, Son.
    After that I'll keep on staying till I dry up and blow away like
    a dessicated mummy."
"I'm planning to write a book too, Dad, The Tectonics of the Colorado
    Plateau. As soon as Heather and I make our fortune here, we're
    going to buy a ranch up in that country."
"Whereabouts in that country?"
70
"Far north of the Mogollon Rim, Dad, far beyond your old ranch, clear
    up in the San Juans. It's got everything, sedimentary formations,
    igneous, metamorphic, minerals, dinosaurs, fossils. We're going
    to take you with us."
"Oh no you're not! I'm a fossil already. Jack and I could never leave
    this country. We *made* this country, doggone it! Our bones belong
    here."

He died on a hot August day when Laura was in San Francisco visiting
    Becky. He telephoned Matt to bring a doctor and come quick, he'd
    been bitten by a rattlesnake.
"Big feller, Matt. Cloudburst must have washed him down the arroyo
    yesterday. Saw him at the bottom of the bank and went for him.
    Slipped right on top of him. Got me in the leg. Hurts like hell."

UNKNOWN EPICS

Emergent evolution, amoeba to paramecium, monkey to man, progress
of people from hereness to thereness!

O promised land, O distant shore, O magnetic allure, more food, more
this, more that, get up and go!

Unknown epics greater than the Iliad and Odyssey, unknown epithets
like unto silver-splashing oars in the wine-dark sea!

Primitive aspirations like unto the sipapu ladder of light out of
the cave of darkness!

Wanderers in the wilderness, builders on the mesa tops, settlers in
the river valleys!

The obviousness of unwritten epics cannot be documented, our most
plausible eisegesis a fallible fantasy.

THE GOLDEN BOUGH

Primordial man was probably as fearless as he was wordless.
Verbality induces fear, superstition, myth, magic, religion
And religion induces contrary beliefs, the counteractive concepts
    of fearless thinkers.
The evolution of ideas is cluttered with solar symbolisms, the sun
    being the source of light and life;
The golden fleece, the golden bough, the golden apples of Hesperides,
    the halos and harps of heaven.
Frazer's golden bough is merely mistletoe, Newton's *Principia* the
    mathematical relation of solar and terrestrial forces,
Written in Latin it is one of the masterpieces of world literature,
    though furtively on the side Newton tried to fit his physics
    into metaphysics,
Gray's *Anatomy* a revelation of man himself, a great anthropology
    with an intrinsic moral regard for the miracle and beauty of
    the human body,
A great graphic poem.

KALI YUGA

The concept of entropy implies the concept of regeneration, syncline
      implies anticline, infinity implies eternity,
And the Yuga time-cycles of Hindu postulation are as credible as
      proterozoic and archaeozoic eras.
Lost civilizations molten back into plutonic slag leave no paleonto-
      logical record whatsoever.
The supposedly decadent Kali Yuga Age in which we live now will last
      only four hundred and thirty-two thousand years leaving no trace,
Unless we orbit an indestructible satellite installed with an inde-
      structible metal television tape tediously transmitting how ludi-
      crously we behaved once upon a time.
Receptivity on any old supersensitive crystalline rock.

ARROWHEAD

If an arrowhead be called a projectile point
Then the arrow must be called a projectile shaft
And the bow a projectile projector.
When a spear is hurled as a javelin
It is certainly projected
But when the same spear is used as a lance
The spearhead is a spearhead.
An atomic warhead is a projectile point,
Feminine logic is a projectile point,
Bubblegum when expectorated is a projectile point
But an arrowhead is the head of an arrow.

SILVER-PINK LOCO WEED

Oxytropis splendens, splendor indeed
The elegant silver-pink loco weed
Bedazzling the daylight, lambert loco too,
Pure white, lavender, lilac, red-blue,
Narcotic for cattle though they usually let it alone
Grazing the creek-cut foothills, the emory oak zone---
Sweet little acorns, edible without leaching,
Main food of the Apaches, Apache country reaching
All along the eastern slope with prairie flowers spread.
They gathered the acorns in baskets, ground them for luscious bread,
Gathered the flowers for color, the silver-pink loco weed
A curious ineffable need

FILAREE

First to come and last to go
Filaree just before snow,
Red-green rosettes on the grey ground,
Pink little flowers shy as the sound
Of dry fallen leaves scudding around.

Cattle next spring will nibble the new
Lush frondescence the winter thaws grew,
Thick flowers develop curled plumes which uncoil
In stiff little spikes to drill in the soil
Re-seeding the range the hoofed herds moil.

VOICES TRAPPED IN LAKE ICE SINGING

A clear sub-zero morning full of snap and zing
We took our little dog around the frozen lake
And stopped surprised on hearing someone sing
Two notes high soprano intensely sad and sweet
All gone, all gone, as if her heart would break.
Then right there at our feet
The droning groan of a baritone so human-sounding near
Our little dog looked up and down and barked almost in fear,
Which seemed to make the lake respond in chorus wailing weird.
Sudden silence, then that high soprano cry
Answered by
Chuttering children's voices as if all gone had reappeared,
Had seen the zingling morning sky
And cheered.

MOUNTAIN MEADOW

At the top of the pass there's a glow in the grass of the mountain
    meadow sloping down from the shadow of aspens and spruce and
    bristlecone pines.
You have to get out and walk in it to see why it shines, flowers
    entangled as thick as vines, color with color intertwines---
Blares of red penstemon and flares of red gilia called scarlet buglers
    and trumpet phlox, three kinds of penstemon three kinds of blue,
    yellow compositae various kinds too,
Wild white cosmos and oxeye daisies, Indian paintbrush brilliant
    red-orange, gayfeather asters called blazing star plumes, blue-eyed
    grass called Sisyrinchium angustifolium.
It's a harmless nomenclature but somewhat fallow midst gentian and
    geum, mimulus and mallow.
Down underneath in the rich meadow loam, too concealed, too profane,
    too cruel for a poem
Root strangles root for water, for food, a constant relentless ruthless
    feud, billions deprived by billions that thrived,
Nobody aware of the throes of despair, nature remorseless as a matter
    of courseness.
But it's nice to survey from the top of the pass, flowers en masse in
    the sheen of the grass.

TRIBUTE TO THE EARTH

ABANDONED BERYL QUARRY
IN NEW HAMPSHIRE

The walls of the old beryl quarry glistened green and lavender with
an inner iridescence when the light struck deep, like the stained
glass windows of a stone church.

It haunted me as a boy, the rubble and shrubbery at the bottom se-
curing its abandonment for my solitary repossession.

Crawl down in the pit of protective glory, the sky comes closer, re-
flection begets reflection, religion is self-containment.

Emerson's gravestone in Sleepy Hollow Cemetery was rough-hewn from
this quarry. It fitted the unitarian spectrum of his thought.

RASBERRY CORDIAL AND DANDELION WINE

Our summer home was a rustic shingle house atop a hill we called
    Spruce Knob, heaven for a small boy.
We had a clear view south to Mt. Monadnock and adown on the lovely
    little stone-walled farms landscaped with elms and hawthorns.
During his one-month vacation from his Philadelphia pastorate my
    father preached in the old Congregational church in the village.
We drove to town Sunday mornings in a two-seated surrey past the
    Brittin farm, Episcopalians, past the Ayre farm, Scotch Presby-
    terians, past the Schiplic farm, Polish Catholics very devout,
    past the Richardson farm, Irish Catholics very vociferous,
And on our way back from church Old Lady Richardson would stand by
    the roadside and shake her bony arm and fist at my father, rail-
    ing him in a dialect I can't reproduce in its full phonetic
    flavor---
"Ye auld heretic ye, cam een faar a sip o' dandelion wine en we'll
    make a dacent Christian o' yet yit!"
My father ecumenically conceded they might convert him into a Cardinal
    Newman someday, and we traipsed in, blueberry cake and a small
    twisty-stemmed goblet of raspberry cordial ready for my partici-
    pation in the communion service.
A childless couple, the Richardsons, fond of animals, fond of people,
    her spontaneous admonitions to my father drolly affectionate.
"Naow that ye have imbibed the juice o' rael religion ye kin fly
    back to yer blitherin auld craow's nest flappin yer black wings
    caw caw cawin about whatcher oughta caw about."

DANCE OF THE SANDHILL CRANES

The haymeadow sloped down to the grassy marshes of the long lake at
the foot of Grand Mesa.
Sandhill cranes congregated there in raucous numbers and celebrated
spring garroo garroo, tuck-luck tuck-luck, onk-konk onk-konk,
Hopped around on their stilt-like legs, craned their crane-like necks,
flapped their clumsy wings like double guitars with a whunk of a
plunk.
It reminded me by contrast of the dancing rabbits I once saw in the
arroyo glade of our Mahualukímo home in New Mexico.
An evening dance, cottontails prescribed, at least a hundred of them,
enough to demolish our garden and strip the bark from the young
fruit trees,
Though nary a one ever munched our carrots or nibbled our lettuce,
preferring alfalfa and filaree, digging under the snow in winter
for them, terpsichorean vitamins no doubt.
A veritable ballet! On hind feet swaying the swirling, front feet
extended like dainty little arms, Nijinsky-like leaps, swimming
in the air, runs, races.
Never in my life had I seen rabbits dance before, my vision confirmed
a few weeks later when our Indian friends Adam Red Deer and Marie
Elk Woman happened on a repeat performance.
I recognized their car coming up our dusty road, a summer evening visit,
but they stopped in the arroyo glade and came no further.
Suspecting motor trouble I walked down to help, found them sitting in
the car spellbound.
Adam put a hush finger to his lips Anglo fashion as I approached,
pointed with his chin Indian fashion toward the glade,
But the rabbits seemed unconcerned about our presence there, dancing
dithyrambic to Tchaikovsky and Stravinsky music for me, Indian
music for Adam and Marie.
"They're like little people!" said Marie with affectionate amusement.
"Never in my whole life do I see rabbit dance like this before!" said
Adam borrowing the English idiom I had felt.
We watched it together fascinated, in rapport with each other as well
as with the rabbits, participating in their ceremony vicariously.
Oh yes, I started to describe the dance of the sandhill cranes. I can
only conclude it is an inferior show compared to that which cotton-
tails produce, though quite superior to the antics of jazz dancers
or rock festival zombies.

84

TAOS EAGLE DANCERS

ROCK OF AGES

Whiter than birch the village church,
A grove of maples behind it dark,
Stood at the edge of the common stark,
Steeple pointing high to the puritan sky,
Belltower stairs leading up to the light
Of the clean white window-bright meeting room,
The stiff-backed pews free for any to choose,
The center aisle as straight as a flume
To the plain oakwood pulpit, reed organ below.
Stand up and sing now, row behind row,
Strong clear sopranos carry the tune
For bass and alto octaves and nasal tenor croon---
Rehear it, rehear it, let memory endear it,
The fervor of those voices as they sang and sang
The old sweet hymns with their old sweet tang,
My faith looks up to thee, thou lamb of calvary
Abide with me, fast falls the eventide
Rock of ages cleft for me---
'Tis salvation of the Me be it he or she,
When the roll is called up yonder I-Me will be there
Climbing up, climbing up the belltower stair.

PALINODE CONCERNING THE ANTHROPOCENTRIC ATTITUDE

There can be no valid religion
Unless the whole scope of life is included in it,
The hawk and the pigeon,
The crow and the linnet,
Bear, wolf, skunk, snake, each for its own sake.
Abraham burnt a ram as a vicarious sham
Rather than sacrifice his son.
Was God's will done?
A man-eating tiger regards man its rightful prey,
Cannibals consider missionaries delectable soufflé,
The shrike kills to kill, like the matador in the bullring, like
        lords and ladies at a foxhunt
Who then go home to guzzle kidney pies and baked fish eyes.
Compassion is the imperative.
Compassion redeems God from notness, religion from rotness,
Spares the spirit it shares.
A terrific spring blizzard drove a bald eagle down to the barbed wire
        fence behind a windbreak of thick-branched box elders and wild
        locust shrubs, our pine-board cabin squaring it off.
Robins and bluebirds perched on the fence, phoebes and magpies, vesper
        sparrows, audubon warblers, doves, swallows.
Beatific interlude. The will to live directs the rapacity of the
        stomach. Bug-eaters, seed-eaters, flesh eaters.
Give us this day our daily bread, meat, drink. Nevertheless and fore-
        most, compassion is the transcendental imperative.

CIRCLE DANCE

PUEBLO FEATHER DANCE

PHARISEES AND SADDUCEES

And lo the Pharisees believed in omens and revelations, in angels of
    the Lord and special dispensations, in retribution, resurrection,
    immortality.
The Sadducees believed only in the freedom of the will to live decently,
    no retribution, no immortality, no preordained fate to render the
    efforts of life absolutely futile.
And the Hindus believed in the ninities of trinities, those cyclical
    threes and threes and threes that devour all good and all evil in
    omnivorous nothingness,
Trimurti Brahma, Vishnu, Siva, trimurti Karma, Samsara, Nirvana, tri-
    murti one plus one plus one equals zero.

FEAR OF LAUGHTER

He excelled at everything he did, a literary intellect, popular pro-
    fessor, ace aviator, golf champion
But he was afraid of laughter and knocked down his serious flights of
    fancy with boomerang wisecracks.
Even in that he excelled, winning the top national prize with a book
    of pungent poems
Which however contained a few hypersensitive sonnets unsullied by
    clever conceits and witty endings.
He ended up himself a schizophrenic puppet in the string-pulling hands
    of the psychiatrist C. G. Jung
Who lacked the discernment and the philosophy of life to cure his fear
    of laughter, or anybody of anything.

THE OYSTER CATCHER'S CRY

On Carmel Point in the 1920's there were just two houses, the Custer
    cottage built of soft yellow limestone set in a wildflower meadow,
    waves of lupine, poppies, suncups, owlclover washing down to the
    waves of the sea.

Jeffers' house was built of rough granite boulders he had lugged up at
    low tide, austerely set on a knoll in a clump of cypresses, wide
    window in the living room, slit windows in the tower room like
    spyholes on the activities of earth, sea, and sky,

Storm crashing cliffs and beaches, mist-magic in the pines on the prom-
    ontories, hawks over the hills, pelicans, gulls, ducks cruising eye-
    level by his tower unto immensity.

He was a thematic ornithologist, Jeffers, and if he happened to be
    rolling boulders up to his house while I happened to be walking
    around the Point we talked birds.

The oyster catcher's shrill piercing cry, louder than surf thunder,
    interrupted conversation, you had to take notice of it.

"It's not a mating call, it's not a natural necessity, there's no
    reason for it," I observed, and could see the grim lines of his
    face draw it inward for a poem.

He came to Taos several seasons, Mabel Luhan's houseguest, so I never
    met him on my birdwalks, but I should have liked to introduce him
    to the northern shrike.

It decoys songbirds with a dulcet song of its own, kills them with one
    stroke of its hooked beak, impales their little bodies on thornbushes,

Its cry more penetrating than the oyster catcher's, one of the most
    fiendish sounds in nature, and there's an intrinsic reason for it.

LEAP OF THE BIGHORN SHEEP

The road was narrow, the precipice steep
Our way was blocked by two bighorn sheep
They glanced at us regally, then gave a leap
Into the canyon four hundred feet deep.
We knelt at the edge to see just where
They'd dropped down the cliff cut sheer and bare
Except for little outcrops like steps in the air
Too far between for a squirrel to dare
But there they stood on good safe ground
Kings of the canyon with coiled horns crowned.

PROSPECTOR'S PALACE

His shack was strong enough to stand the heaviest snow
Mountains all around it, sunset peaks aglow
Plenty of firewood, plenty of water dipped from the thermal spring
Plenty of hope, no telling what each day would bring
Digging in his hillside tunnel, hard work kept him warm
Despite the wildest winter storm.
In summer it was paradise replete with pine and spruce
Dazzling alpine meadows, the flowers so profuse
He gathered big bouquets and took them into town---
Penstemons red and blue and dusky purplish brown
Mertensia, jasmine, gentian, maple-leafed hollyhocks
Campanula, paintbrush, primrose, long-lasting trumpet phlox
Mariposa lilies delicate mauve white---
And gave them to the ladies, inimitably polite
A huge-framed iron-armed Swede who never swore and never drank
Never got in a fight, for which lesser men could thank
Gentle and generous to everyone, his eyes a smoky blue
Anna, deez forget-me-nots I pick dem joos for you
Summertime was prospect time in his secret gulch of gold
Hoard the precious nuggets, smaller stuff quietly sold
Get rich and marry Anna, go round the world and back
Or just stay here from year to year in your windproof worldproof shack.

ALCHEMY

In the Cresson vug at Cripple Creek
Crystals of gold replaced crystals of quartz
Alchemy the ancients tried to eke
Out of duller metals of baser sorts

Scientists alchemize elements today
By electric and chemical interplay.
But no magician can change biologically
A self to a self, or even psychologically.
Granted the growth from young to old
The identity we hold is stronger than gold.

Nor is insanity a transfer of personality;
Your delusion you are Napoleon isn't Napoleon in you,
It's your idea of Napoleon, the name, the fame in crazy context,
Your subconscious self writhing in terrible torment.

Reincarnation likewise is a verbal conceit;
What qualities after death do you wish to repeat?
Okay, buddy, go ahead and transmigrate,
You'll find your identity difficult to reincorporate.
And to hypnotize a man to believe himself a saint
Is very very quaint but he really knows he ain't.

THE VERBAL IMAGE

I saw the score of a symphony in a dream, saw the notes, heard the
  sounds vivid, glorious, thrilling,
Great arpeggios rolling vertical up the staffs, soaring melodic lines
  descending in rich tone-cluster harmonies, crescendo dissonances
  resolved in lovely legatos.
It vanished when I awoke, unreproducible, but it still sticks in my
  memory an ecstatic experience.
Analyzing the actuality of it I concluded the verbal image is the mother
  of the visual image and tonal image.
What I dreamed I saw and heard was evoked by the names *score, symphony,*
  note, staff, the rolling *arpeggios* were *dominant ninths G B D F A-flat,*
  ghost names catalytic of ghost sight-sounds. Pitch.
Which is why Beethoven could conceive his later compositions though
  deaf, I'll do a sonata in C minor in two movements.
Which is why an artist paints a portrait by word application, *curve* of
  eyebrows, slant of *eyes,* what *color* are her eyes, not *brown,* not
  hazel, topaz, that's it, *topaz,* how the dickens do I paint *topaz?*
  Nuclear physicists proceed by verbal concepts to mathematical symbols,
  counter concepts, counter symbols, ideographs.
The Egyptians constructed their gods by associate concepts, false similes,
  Ra, Horus, Hathor, Sibu, Nuit, Osiris, Isis, Thoth the god of wisdom,
  a baboon.

NECROPHILIA

Women came by the carload
To throw themselves on his grave,
His ashes mixed with cement
So none could dig down and steal some.
They beat their heads on the pine-needles,
Tapped their toes in the turf,
Weird necrophilia wriggling above
The dust of the man who never knew love.

MELANCHOLIA

Darkness and void and dead desire
Gone is the glow of the living fire
Instruments, measurements, rules of behaving
Futility, despair, Dürer's engraving.

THE SENSE OF POSSESSING, SENSE OF BELONGING

Two little half-sisters Daisy and Rose, and their eight-year-old half-
    brother Robert, just Robert.
Children of the universe, their mother not knowing who their fathers
    were, fertilized by the winds of wanderlust.
It wrenched your heart just to look at just Robert, his lost eyes be-
    seeching you, wanting to be wanted, his shy smile fearing your re-
    vulsion, rabbity teeth needing a dentist's care.
And the two little girls were dirtier and smellier than he, Daisy's
    sick clammy complexion and sick filmy eyes horribly pathetic, Rose
    a defiant redhead inured to adult promiscuity, her hard green eyes
    craved innocence.
The cure is possessive love, protective love, constancy, someone and
    something to claim one's own, to belong to, be true to.
The crime is irresponsible breeding, the poem is pity for every forlorn
    waif born to the multiple millions.

PACHYSTIMA

At Christmas time in California the evergreens were huckleberry
    and toyon
And fragrant fronds of redwood wreathes
And you heard the wrentits and songsparrows singing in the toyon
    thickets
The russet-backed thrush in the redwood groves.
Here in the Rockies the evergreens are the branch-tips of the Douglas
    fir, symbol of everlasting life to the Indians,
And the deep forest groundcover Pachystima myrsinites called mountain
    myrtle
And you hear the hermit thrush and kinglets singing in the pine, fir
    and spruce trees
The water-ouzel on the stream-splashed rocks banked with mountain
    myrtle.

YUCCA MOTH

Dainty white moth in the white yucca bell
Mimetic whiteness, symbiotic rightness.
Blackness isn't evil, coal is as pure as snow
Night is not oblivion, as any moth would know.
Every isness has its shell
Too mysterious to tell.

FETISH

Feel the smooth carved fetish, it assures good luck.
Feel the contour of a mountain, the firm familiar outline, the singing
　　ringing skyline, it assures the place you live.
Beargod fetish, deer, turtle, coyote, the sungod image sacrosanct, a
　　dangerous deceit, beware its human sacrifice.
The sun is the sun, photosynthesis the source of life, photosynthesis
　　of primordial chemicals, primordial protoplasm, virgin birth, mother
　　and child
Mystic marvelous tangible reality, no fetish so reassuring as the broad
　　green leaf.

WHATEVER OUR FINAL FATE

Reconsider the kiva of conformity of belief
The sipapu outlet inlet symbolic
Release, return, seek a true way.
Vulgarize the symbol psychedelic escape
Dope drink sex
Lost in lurid lovelessness.

Life itself is the grace of God
Miracle of seed in the common clod
Miracle of love greater than seed
Instilling soul like a flower's breath
In brute desire and physical need
Song in the heart more durable than death.

Fusion of love with the sting of brain
Aspire aspire, attain attain
Infinite realization in the infinite instant
Certitudes as close as the stars are distant.
The way is clear, then, far free elate
Whatever our final fate.

ABOUT THE AUTHOR

PHILLIPS KLOSS was born in Webster Groves, Missouri in 1902.
Moving to New Mexico in 1916, where he worked on his brother's ranch,
he later graduated from the University of California in Berkeley in 1925.
Mr. Kloss, once a reporter on the San Francisco Bulletin, married the artist/etcher
Alice Geneva Glasier (Gene Kloss) and moved to Taos, New Mexico in 1927
where he still lives.
He is the author of several other books of poetry and maintains an avid interest
in Western ethnology and nature.
The present volume is a religious essence of his country and his humanity
with the kiva theme, the mana theme and the verbality theme consistent throughout.

ABOUT THE ARTIST

GENE KLOSS, a member of the National Academy, is considered to be
among the best etchers in the world.
Her faithful record of the spirit and ceremony of the Pueblo Indian is valued,
not only by collectors, but also by anthropologists who use her work
to verify costume and dance.
In a career that spans more than fifty years in Taos, New Mexico
during the literary and artistic heyday of the twenties, as well as in
Carmel, California during the halcyon times of Jack London and company,
Gene Kloss is a tribute to the dedication of her craft.
Art critic Alfred Frankenstein stated:
"She is both poet and virtuoso,
but the virtuosity is always kept subordinate to the poetic ideal."

THE GREAT KIVA

Book design by Mina Yamashita Balleydier
at The Sunstone Press
in Santa Fe, New Mexico.

Printed on Ivory Scott Book and set in Paladium,
a typeface designed by Hermann Zapf
and adapted for Compugraphic.
A limited edition of
500 are bound in English Buckram and are
numbered and signed by the Author and Artist.

www.ingramcontent.com/pod-product-compliance
Lightning Source LLC
Chambersburg PA
CBHW080539090426

42733CB00016B/2632